"Yvette Neisser Moreno's poems shimmer in that mysterious space between rib and spine, body and sky, farewell and departure. This is where she seeks equilibrium. She brings the same discipline and elegance to her poems as she does to dance and calligraphy."
— Barbara Goldberg, author of *The Royal Baker's Daughter*

"With quiet precision and evocative narratives that take us from lovely Hussein smoking a sheesha after losing his sight to an inner landscape of the Great Pyramid and a passage into eternity with its endless, circling shades of deeper blue, Yvette Neisser Moreno takes us on a journey where the senses are the compass for being present in the world. This fine first book of poems takes us along the uncharted spaces between the body and the experience of the world, calling us into its winding, into the warmth and joy of its eloquent movements. The poet draws us up close and releases us into our own bodies, our own mindful breath."
— Naomi Ayala, author of *This Side of Early*

" 'Some of us live at a slant,' the poet Yvette Neisser Moreno writes in *Grip* and then proceeds to show us how, in language soothing and startling, both. The poems are 'a slow plea/for the beating of human hearts,' whether among the conflicts and struggles of the Middle East or within a single family or a single one of us wrestling with her grief. These are poems of great humanity. Read them for their crystalline truths and for the joy they find in our difficult hearts."

—Sarah Browning, director of the organization Split This Rock and author of *Whiskey in the Garden of Eden*

"From the horrors of the Holocaust to the grace of plié, from the pyramids of Egypt to her father's passing, Yvette Neisser Moreno's noble voice in *Grip* explores the 'arc out of thinking' between a dawn that 'trembles with faint prayers' and death like a 'fluidity of grain.' Neisser Moreno's yearning for comprehension and her pristine sensitivity 'grip' the reader from the start. In her delicate poems she reminds us that strength rises from understanding and that poetry, at its core, is always a way to 'untwist language from dreams.' Enter the 'stillness before snow,' the compelling landscape of this extraordinary collection."

—Clifford Bernier, judge and author of *The Silent Art*

Grip

Poems by

Yvette Neisser Moreno

Arlington, Virginia

Published by Gival Press, an imprint of Gival Press, LLC.

For information please write:
Gival Press, LLC
P. O. Box 3812
Arlington, VA 22203
www.givalpress.com

First edition
ISBN: 978-1-92-8589-76-1
eISBN: 978-1-928589-78-5
Library of Congress Control Number: 2012942441

Photo of Yvette Neisser Moreno by Allison R. Kokkoros.
Design by Ken Schellenberg.
Art cover: © Alkestis | Dreamstime.com

Acknowledgments

Grateful acknowledgment is made to the editors of the publications in which the following poems, sometimes in earlier versions, first appeared:

Attic: "The Armoire" (2007)

Beltway Poetry Quarterly: "How the Water Settles" (Winter 2011); "Line by Line" (published as "Connecting the Dots"), "Mockingbird," and "Nocturnal Life" (Spring 2011); "The Slow Passage to Anacostia" (Summer 2006 and Fall 2008)

Foreign Policy in Focus: "A Question of Friendship" (July 2011)

Gargoyle: "Languages I Have Learned" (2008)

Innisfree Poetry Journal: "Grief" (March 2006) and "Juliek's Violin" (September 2005)

Loch Raven Review: "After a Funeral" (Summer 2011)

North Carolina Literary Review: "The Clouds Barely Make It" (published as "Out of the Water," 2002)

Potomac Review: "Walden Pond, Before Dusk" (published as "Before Dusk, The Pond in Fog," Fall/Winter 2005-06)

Praxilla: "Finding the Way" (published as "From the Shadows," October 2009)

Seventh Quarry: "Mantra to Untwist Language from Dreams" and "Night in the Desert" (Summer 2011)

Slide: "Between Farewell and Departure" and "Birds in Flight" (Fall 2000)

Tar River Poetry: "In Plié" (Spring 2004)

Virginia Quarterly Review: "Ashes and Shooting Stars" (published as

"Eighth Grade") and "Shades of Dawn" (Winter 2000).

The following poems first appeared in the following publications.

"Now, Anything Can Quicken Your Heartbeat" appeared in *September Eleven: Maryland Voices*, edited by Rosemary Klein (9/11 Project/ Baltimore Writers' Alliance, 2002).

"Dusk on the Ridge" appeared in *Poetic Voices Without Borders*, edited by Robert L. Giron (Gival Press, 2005).

"Cairo" (published as "A Deluge of Script") and "In the Valley of the Kings" appeared in *Poetic Voices Without Borders 2*, edited by Robert L. Giron (Gival Press, 2009).

"The Slow Passage to Anacostia" also appeared in *Full Moon on K Street: Poems about Washington, DC*, edited by Kim Roberts (Plan B Press, 2010).

I also would like to express my deepest gratitude to the following wonderful people who provided invaluable comments on the manuscript and/or individual poems: Lavonne Adams, Naomi Ayala, Sandra Beasley, Sarah Browning, Mark Cox, Patricia Bejarano Fisher, Emily Francomano, Bernadette Geyer, Katherine Howell, Judy Neri, Bonnie Nevel, Katy Richey, Joanna Robin, Darcy Shargo, Frank Tascone, and Katherine Young.

But most importantly, I could not have completed this book without the undying support of my mother, Joan Neisser, and my husband, Jorge Moreno. Thank you for helping me bring this dream to fruition.

Finally, I am grateful to the teachers whose guidance and insights on poetry have stayed with me through the years: Carolyn Forché, Marie Howe, Philip Levine, David Rivard, Dennis Sampson, and Michael White.

Contents

I

THE TREMBLE OF FAINT PRAYERS

The Stillness before Snow

This, not spring, is the time of beginnings.
A celestial hush has descended,
wrenching the wind to stillness,
startling birds back to their roosts,
beaks clamped shut
to empty the moment of sound.
Everything suspended. The air
rests in my hands.

And in the sky, all shades of white,
ivories and chalk-whites and dove-feathers
blending and unblending,
released from an artist's palette
onto this moving canvas.

The holiness of these hours
as we wait for a vision.

The world loosens its hold on the sky,
unclenches frozen fields
from their winter shapes,
and snow fills the night
as if it had always been coming.

This requires prayer, and the belief
that all the rifts in earth could cohere again
with the salve of these soft flakes,
that even jagged watermarks
etched in stone like a story of despair
could be unwritten in throes of white.

Juliek's Violin

After Night, *by Elie Wiesel*

Afraid of dying without it, he ran forty miles
clutching it beneath his shirt—
just keep it warm,
keep the wood from cracking.

Caught in the momentum of men
hurling their bodies forward
into the ranks of snow, he trampled fathers
who sank into the white grave underfoot.

The night's blizzard and cold
deafened his belief in beauty. White
now the color of unending nightmares.
Snow, a negation of future.

After humming his way through fumes
that permeated dreams and clung
to his body, imbuing him
with the scent of his own death,

it was there, in that empty-hearted night,
stumbling along the fragile trajectory
between collapse and existence—
the cacophony of barking dogs
nearly consumed his internal melodies.

But Juliek kept hold of his violin,
fingers bleeding into the maple's grain.

Abandoned factory:
men piling one on another to sleep or die,
whichever might come first.
Though he *could hardly breathe*
beneath the pressure of somebody's back,
he scratched his way out
from the smother of bodies,
violin's neck in his fist,
bow sheltered in the crook of his arm.

Unsure if he still could create sound,
Juliek navigated the instrument
through the stiffening air
until his chin found the place to rest.
He angled the bow to fathom each string
and pulled a concerto, note by note,
from the hollow vessel: a slow plea
for the beating of human hearts.

Now, Anything Can Quicken Your Heartbeat

after September 11, 2001

Now, anything can quicken your heartbeat—
the rush of a train, a dog's bark,
the sudden rustle of leaves
as a bird flies out of a bush,

night's utter silence, the dark rooms
and vulnerability of windows.
Still, on the holiest day of the year,
wax drips down a candelabra

from seven burning candles,
forming spontaneous patterns
around the brass of each branch,
one drop layered upon another;

and the flames, those minute glimpses
into the soul, flutter like stars
before they vanish
as if closing from within.

After the shofar blows,
after the prayers for the unfound dead
trapped under the smoldering remains
of our once unwavering landscape,

something is left:
the elegant sweepings of wax,
a testament to the fire they once contained,
to the permanence of a pure, ragged beauty.

The Words of the Script

You kept to yourself
as immigrant fathers are inclined to do,
kept your first life twined in your first language,
not translating the years knotted in secrets,

not unfolding the documents,
not unwrapping the old menorah
from its crumpled paper, not emerging
from behind the shell of father.

Now, we glean remnants of your life
from what you left behind:
a beige overcoat, collar partly turned up,
a felt hat stiffened by wind and sweat,
a framed Yiddish poster announcing
your starring role in *King Lear*.

In the last weeks of rehearsal
you shuffled from room to room
mumbling lines, now and again blurting out
> *Is man no more than this?*
> *See how this world goes with no eyes . . .*

Brief riddles, proverbs, snatches of prayer
culled from the words of the script:
> *We cry that we are come to this great stage of fools . . .*

Was it some rhythm in these words
that broke your silence,
loosening the seams of untold stories
you had raveled deep in your memory?

I will not swear these are my hands . . .

And how would you recognize yourself?
When you've had to do unbelievable things—
bury your family menorah, pray
you'd get out and find it again;

when you've ridden a freight train
through a countryside radiant with tulips,
red petals emboldened by sunlight
as if all those years, the world
had seen nothing but beauty,
until finally you had to jump,
chase a stray chicken's yellow feathers
and tear its head from its neck;

when you've seen a man starve himself
because he refused to eat soup with horsemeat—

you'll do anything for his sake,
you'll eat whatever you can,
you will find joy.

Shades of Dawn

a dialogue with García Lorca

What would you call this,
after the sky has huddled
around a half-sun on the horizon?

Aurora, maybe?

If the dawn is very close to the soul,
worshippers kneeling at the water's edge,
waiting for God to rise in the mist,

if it silvers wet sand like the inside
of a shell, and the ocean scoops out
uncolored spaces from the low tide,

is that *alba*?

Once the sun pinks the water,
and the day begins to open—
the space between dawn and day

when everyone is sleepwalking,
when the houses have softened
their edges in morning's blur—

if a man floats in a bed of waves,
toes pointing up, hands folded,
has he achieved *madrugada*? Or *amanecer*?

Federico, how can I write
when dawn can never end with a vowel
and every daybreak trembles with faint prayers?

The Line between River and Ocean

for A. H. T.

At the sun's highest hour, we fumbled
for hand-holds—ocean smacking wet stone,
pouring into the cracks of crumbling sea wall,
white water pummeling our thighs—
and I kept thinking, this would be some death,
a gradual saturation, the river creeping into us
one limb at a time, our last moments measured
by the ferry chugging from one port to the other.

Of the two of us, I knew you would survive—
you could swim your way out of a flood if you had to.

As I groped on hands and knees all the way back,
shedding my belongings into a rising sea,
you balanced in the spaces between rocks,
proceeding notch by notch along the sinking jetty,
steadying yourself with one hand, and with the other,
holding our bag of apples above the water,
just a few drops from the spray
splashing closer and closer to your fist.

Ashes and Shooting Stars

The year Chris and Matt died on the tracks
I cut my hair short and grew it long again,
Mandi stopped talking to me three times,
the Challenger blew up.

The only year of my life when I brushed blue
over eyelids and lined my eyes in black,
the year of spinning bottles to see who
would kiss with lips and who with tongues,

the year they built the planetarium
and every day, two o'clock meant the descent
to a world of swirling darkness
where we leaned back to let galaxies
haze our eyes. I never thought the sky
could really look like that, black
and full of flickering life.

That year, diesels cranked through my sleep,
peppering it with ashes and shooting stars.
I kept waking up wanting to tell somebody—
you can't lie down on the tracks
and expect to live.

That didn't stop the broken reel
from replaying the scene I imagined:
Chris and Matt rising as the train comes,
arms and legs spread in a big X—
then the impact against their palms
scatters their paired lives across the universe,
breaking open that bare light.

Mantra to Untwist Language from Dreams

Let sleep have no language,
let it have only color,
deep purple,
let it have the shape of a mountain at dusk
or the span of an eagle's wing.

Let it have an undercurrent,
the cadence of the heart,
let it have sound, but no voices,
let it pulse, let it thrum,
let moonlight seep into it,
let dreams dissolve into one long hum.

Let the mountain heave me on its back
and smooth me over its peak

or let me be the mountain,
rock-still,
the earth beating beneath me.

Insomnia

I am kept awake by two tall stems
outside my window, vigilant
and aching toward the sky.

The whole night is shaken
by their green ascendance,
each one tipped by a pair of leaves
in a cupped V.

Is this the posture I should dream in—
body fixed to the ground,
arms extending upward,
each hand's four fingers
facing their thumb? Tell me

my palms can form such a vessel
to carry me through to morning.

Tell me about the unflinching curve of leaves
holding their own soft weight.

II

BIRDS IN FLIGHT

Birds in Flight

Opa's baby grand stood by the window,
holding the room in place.

Here, his sons played duets through childhood—
Fred cradling his viola,
elbow lifted like a bird's wing
above my father's fingers on the keys—

and Opa traversed oceans,
gathering silks for Oma from the Far East.

***

Nineteen years were enough for Fred
to understand the world, for life
to overtake him from the inside,
for a bottle of poison to be emptied
into his welcoming body.

The pages of his final letters
were hurried into a bottom drawer,
his death absorbed by the density of oak,
the lush fibers of Persian rugs.

Oma wrapped her grief around her
with long colored scarves and fur-lined coats.

Only the piano was left
to keep my father company.
Some days, Opa propped open the top
so hammers and strings glinted in the sun.

***

Over the years, the Blüthner's legs had scribed
three dents in the rug.

Oma had long ago lain down on the bed
of her lost son, to enter death
in the warmth of his presence.

My father delved into concertos
while I cut dolls from their outlines
and Opa sipped his steaming tea,
nodding to those long-fingered melodies
and telling stories of condors
soaring above the Andes,
his voice unfurling each feather
to shelter us under six-foot wings.

***

When Opa died, heirlooms migrated
to our living room: the plaster bust of Oma,
some keys to unlock the scrolling desk,
a wooden carving of birds in flight,
the old piano, a flutter of teabags,
Oma's silks folded inside the piano bench
with sheet music of Brahms and Mozart.

And a black-and-white photo:
a little girl, curls tucked in a barrette,
watching Opa pour cream into his tea.

Her teacup has yet to be filled.

Gliding Through This Place

Hiroshima, 1955

In her hospital bed, Sadako folds
one thousand paper cranes.

She uses every spare paper she can find:
candy wrappers, scraps nurses leave behind,
prescription slips, pages from magazines.
Her fingers crease perfect triangles,
lengthen necks, pinch little beaks,
pull open the wide wings of hope,
then she hangs them everywhere,
decorating ceilings and windows
until flocks of cranes flood the hallways.

Each crane is a triumph in the race
against the white blood cell count. As the days
and blood tests stack up against her
like the war that attacked this city
and keeps pounding its people with illness,
she defies the onslaught of pain
coursing through her body,
defies a world of nuclear rain
with these birds of transcendence.

Rainy season falls dark and hard
over the hospital wing. But the cranes
flutter and rustle, keeping their poise,
heads lifted and wings spread
as if gliding through this place
en route to somewhere else,

anywhere that children do not die,
anywhere they can carry Sadako
to run beneath the open sky.

Radiance

After Ray Bradbury, "All Summer in a Day"

No birds fly here.
Margot's waking hours measured
by the seconds between lightning bolts,
the lulls between downpours.
Always the sky pressing down,
always water smashing against windows,
even her dreams darkened by rain.

All these wet years, the promise of sun
has sustained her like the glow of God
under the rubble of war,
until one glorious day:
the drops finally taper
and the first rays trickle through.

The other children lock her
in the coatroom, then burst out
into sunlight's wild exuberance.

After hurling her tiny body
against the pitiless door,
Margot strains to reach the window,
stretching against the wall
until her fingers turn white,
until she can't feel her toes.
She wants at least a touch
of heat on her palms.

With each tick of the clock,
she watches flecks of light
shimmer along the window frame,
pulls hangers from the coat rack
one by one, tracing the circumference
of each hook tinged with sun.

As day closes, the sun's descent
will radiate streaks of fire,
pink flames and red embers.

If only she could trap that radiance,
tuck it in her pocket—like a drinker
with a flask of brandy, or a soldier
with a lover's photo—she might survive
the next seven years of rain.

After a Funeral

In the middle of hide-and-seek,
we found ourselves staring into the closet:
suits, starched shirts, empty shoes.
Though Uncle Lenny was gone,
his loafers were polished,
closet door ajar, wooden pipe
still lying on the dresser.
                              Just a moment
face to face with closet darkness,
then we were back in the game
dashing from room to room
to look for hiding places.

Only this morning, pulling my coat
around my shoulders, it came to me—
there was a man who once stood
in those huge, gaping shoes,
whose wrists once filled those hollow cuffs.
Poppy, my cousins called him.
So he was somebody's husband,
somebody's brother. Somebody.

Mockingbird

Wobbling between shade and sun,
a lone bird steps toward us, then stops;
opens its beak, but no sound comes.

This must be the end of life:
a bird that no longer flies,
a voice that no longer speaks.

We, the survivors, feel his solitude,
feel the wings shudder with effort.
This bird shall not be forgotten.

This bird shall remain tottering
at the edge of memory,
reminding us of what comes next.

Between Farewell and Departure

Opa held my hand as far as the sign
Passengers only beyond this point
then nudged me toward the long hallway
where my first solo journey would begin.

I glanced back for one last image of his face
that I could carry with me like a compass.

Airports and train stations were as familiar to him
as home—having lived on three continents,
he was attuned to the nuances of verbs,
to accents and lilts in speech,
each language a symphony,
words and sounds arranging themselves
until vowels harmonized into meaning.

For me, the distance from one coast to another
was still a mystery, full of clouds and turbulence,
and my life was just beginning to take off
as I reached the plane door.

Among the gates and waiting passengers,
I could hear Opa's echo
in the mirage of voices around me—
adults who seemed to know some secret
of the world I had yet to understand.

As long as memory exists,
he will be there, waving to me
on the border between farewell and departure,
about to disappear once I round the end of the corridor.

III

NIGHT IN THE DESERT

Night in the Desert

Had I been spun around blindfolded
and dropped into the salt
of a huge shattered hourglass?
Dizzied by the sheen of sand,
I had entered a world
where space is uncountable,
where I could orient myself only
by the relation of sky to earth.

All that sand piled
from the earth's core to the surface
formed a berth beneath my back,
something I could lean on
to stop the spinning.

And the stars spread before me,
each one straining for the outer reaches
of illumination, tensed and attuned
like a muscle contracting,
like the inner stretch of the soul
pushing against the edges
of its own circumference.

Cairo

The junk man's song floated over Cairo
like driftwood—every morning I listened
to its rise and fall and didn't understand,
its three flat notes tumbling along with me
past the empty bench outside my building,
past a vendor rolling a wagon of green figs,
their smooth skin pocked by thorns,
past the mangos in mesh bags
above the juicer's stall, past the hint
of open doorways, the scent of frying chickpeas
and oil sizzling in metal vats,
past boys on bicycles
balancing trays piled with bread,
past the hunched back of one man,
spine curved like a perfect horseshoe,
head below his shoulders.

Submerged in a sea of Arabic, a deluge of script.
On every building, every billboard,
letters looped together right to left, saying something
just beyond my grasp.

First Glimpse of the Pyramids

My journey nearly paralleled
    the journey of dusk,
        that strange winding path

from daylight to darkness—
    how blue softens to lilac,
        then indigo—

until finally, at the brink
    of desert and city,
        there they were:

three pinnacles
    demarcating the sky
        and steadying the earth

with their crumbling brick,
    the color of burnished cedar,
        those perfect angles

that held the course
    of the universe twined
        in their ancient mathematics.

In the Wadi

For hours through that valley of red peaks,
Ayed navigated the jeep over sand,

tires tracking within the mountains' bounds
as though the route were well-trodden.

He tried to tell me a story about a snake,
about a night sleeping out in the gorge—

Arabic nouns and verbs scattered in my mind,
weaving a pattern, a sketch of the story,

but I couldn't understand the stitches,
the secret of living the desert every day,

of breathing these red mountains into the night,
sheltered by a ceiling of rock formations.

I shook my head. He gave up,
pushed a cassette into the tape deck

to let a woman's quivering voice permeate
our silence with the rise and fall of octaves.

As if she had swallowed some of that desert space,
her vast song narrowed the expanse

between the jeep and the heart
of the wadi. Afternoon slowly melted

into the mountains' tender core,
and we climbed up crag by crag

to glimpse the sun lowering itself
beyond a dark apex. Finally,

a communication I knew. A turn of color:
blue sky reddened, red mountains blackened

in relief against a pink backdrop,
so I could trace the contours with a finger.

A Question of Friendship

Something tender about skin
and muscle framed by ancient stone.

The pyramids behind us in silhouette,
solid, rooted, entirely diagonal.

The night deepened,
the city's glimmer distant.

Fadi drew on his smoke.
Do you support Israel?

I took a deep breath,
listened to the desert hum,

felt the weight of silence.
Would the night weave my love

for Israel and Palestine
into some kind of logic?

I hoped the truth would be enough.
Yes, and the Palestinian cause.

Time stopped ticking
as I waited for an answer:

his half-smoked cigarette
flung from mouth to sand,

that flick of the wrist,
straightening of the elbow,

and the glint of that tiny fire
shimmering against the darkness.

Alright, he said.

We walked on into the long night,
wending down an unmarked path.

Smoke

Holding in one hand the checkered tube
that carried tobacco up from burning red coals,
from water bubbling in glass below,
Hussein slowly exhaled through pursed lips.

After losing his vision, this became his art:
forming swirls of smoke
that hung above his dark glasses
in long, curved shapes
like the outlines of a dream.

The Slow Ferry

It had been hours since departure,
pushing off into the quiet waters
between countries, ferry tilling
the unturned surface, folding back
a layer of sea. At the time for prayer,
one man laid his carpet on the deck
and others joined, crowding their fabrics
to form the beginnings of a quilt.

Soon, there were forty men praying
in the middle of the Red Sea:
standing to face the east,
then in unison on their knees,
foreheads to the floor, and up again—
Allahu akbar, a chorus carried
on the billowing breeze.

That night, I sat up on deck,
floating under the stars.
On shore, beneath two palm trees,
a fire burned—the only light for miles,
a spark in the night. We all have
our own way of yearning.

Moulid: Night of the Prophet

Night captured in the flicking tongues
of women outside the mosque,
sleeping babies in their laps.
Hands cupped above their upper lips,
their shrill voices formed a canopy

over two rows of men in a moving
meditation: eyes closed, torsos swinging
as the *tabla* player beat out the trance,
his flat palm sounding the stretched skin
of a drum, his voice a mesmeric hum
intoning the chants of the prophets.

Every few minutes, one man or another
lost hold of the rhythm's mesh,
spinning out in private transcendence
until someone pulled him to a doorway,
splashing water on his face.

The mosque was empty. But its windows
were wide open, letting in
the trills of the women below.

Black-Out

Even the mosquitoes were stilled
when the garden lights blinked out,
plunging us into darkness: guests hushed
by the descent of a vast sky
blotting out remnants of conversation
and eclipsing the swish of brandy,
fervent stars dimming
the glowing ends of cigarettes.

Just then, the pyramids surfaced,
forging their angles
onto the blank desert air.

For the rest of the night,
they hovered at the edge of vision,
darker than the dark.

Scent

From the night breeze came a howling
that blended in and out of the wind,
fixing me to the spot—

wild dogs
kicking up torrents of sand,
green eyes luminous as shards of glass.

I was so conscious of being human,
the desert lighting my skin,
lifting my scent on the wind.

But they skirted me, crossing through
the film of semi-lit darkness
that marked the limits of my sight.

Wild dogs rising out of the desert
and disappearing back into it, as in a vision,
that moment of panting, then gone.

Perhaps I had no scent at all.
Perhaps I had become part of the landscape.

Dusk on the Ridge

The air was dense, filled
with the flames of small fires
and the scent of roasting corn.

Too late to see the pyramids
or the domes of minarets, now obscured
by the oncoming night. But there below,
in one dry curve of the valley
was a rift between two hills,
their contours blurred
by the jumble of light and dark.

Caught in the sway
of those shifting shadows,
I felt suddenly weightless
as if I were falling into that dip
or suspended on a pendulum
swinging hypnotically
in the space between two solids.

Something opened up
in the unmoving earth,
something unsteadied.

Inside the Great Pyramid

The slant of the inner wall
forced me to ascend into history
in a slow half-crawl, to humble myself
before reaching the dead king, or his spirit.

Like the pyramid's heart, the room was bare—
a single light bulb strung
above one empty coffin. But the pressure
of limestone and centuries had distilled the air

so I could see each particle, alive and moving,
and imagine the king's spirit hovering there
as devotees brought offerings of wine and fruit
to sustain him in the world of the dead.

I wanted to stay there through the night,
palm touching stone, forearm like a chain
linking my body with that wall
of granite, steeped in time.

The Unfinished Obelisk

It lay on its side in the quarry,
surface already sanded,
not yet hewn from the stone beneath.
Between itself and the rock that birthed it
were thousands of chisel marks, each the shape
of a spatula's motion, scraping
a ridged channel from the quarry wall
to the obelisk's edge.

One narrow crack
zagged down the finished side.

They must have spent weeks, perhaps months
crafting that stone—then, seeing the imperfection,
moved on, leaving their unfinished art
to shift the world's tilt just a notch.

In the Valley of the Kings

I liked to imagine the artists there on ladders,
paintbrushes dipped in azurite, covering the ceiling
of the tilted entranceway with the blue
of a night sky, patched with yellow stars.
Their pigments filled every inch
of those walls leading to the tomb.
A language of pictures—beetle, horned viper,
a jagged line, an arm bent at the elbow,
hieroglyphs cutting slices of story
into the sequence of friezes
pushing forward across the walls,
one scene feeding into another
in the manner of life or memory:
boys yoking a bull to sacrifice,
men fishing the Nile, a woman kneeling,
pounding bread on a flat stone.
An offering of incense scrolls
into a procession of chariots rolling
toward some unseen destination
and so on down to the wall's cracked edge,
down to the burial chamber.

The journey of the sun beneath the earth ends there
on the ceiling above the tomb, in a deep blue,
the color of the sea leading to death—
Day and Night facing each other,
volleying the sun
along the length of their bodies.

This is how I picture the passage
to eternity: an endless circling
into deeper and deeper shades of blue.

IV

UNCHARTED SPACES

Finding the Way

for Jorge

From the shadows of this hidden town,
the buried pulse of front porches and empty rockers,
the trunks of live oaks whose soft leaves canopy our streets,
from wisteria coiled like wire around these pines,
dangling chains of tiny purple blossoms, from the absolute
mystery of seeds multiplying in soil,

from under the weight of fishing piers, wooden columns riveted
by water's burden, from the tide lashing upward,
all echo and spray, from the frail lines trailing
their hooks along the ocean's spume,
from the indented cradle between two waves,

from a lizard's darting glance, the slow creak
of the drawbridge opening its jaws to the ebbing sun,
from the yellow skim coating the river,
the traces of moon over my backyard,
the freight train's midnight wail, the narrow space
between two notes of a wind chime,
the long swallow of language—

From all this, you found your way to love me?

How the Water Settles

When I was a child,
there was a net I feared falling into—
people caught in a tumult of ropes,
climbing a few steps
then tumbling back down,
unable to grip something
so full of holes. I clung to the rim
as if I could remain solid
by holding onto that wood.

These nights, I dream of rivers,
the two of us in a small canoe:
a congestion of boats,
hull knocking against hull,
we rock in the wake.

Awakening in your embrace,
sometimes I run my fingers
along the length of your arm,
trying to trace my future
in the patterns of veins that fade
into the crook of your elbow.

After the world shakes on its axis,
there you are, steadying me,
absorbing all that friction.
The water settles.
The earth realigns.

In Plié

for Melvin Deal

Each bang of the drum pushes my focus
further down the body: vertebrae aligned
along the spine, knees bent in second position,
feet firm on the floor.

> *Lower! Deeper!* Melvin's voice
> permeates the room as I descend

again and again into plié,
muscles quivering to support me.
The mind wanders into its own mirror,
reflecting the blur of thoughts

> like a disordered alphabet,
> then, that emptiness.

With repetition, there comes an awareness
of quadriceps. They announce their presence
like bands of color stretching from knee to hip,
deepening into the flicker of violet

> the longer I hold this position. *The strength
> of the body is in the thighs*, Melvin says.

This is why we do half our movements in plié—
from plié comes the jump,
the circling of arms, fluidity of spine,
hands offered open-palmed to the audience—

      from the dip into plié comes the dip
      into the mind, the arc out of thinking,

from the bending of knees comes
a spring to the surface
of consciousness, that uncharted space
between body and sky.

Line by Line

The day blurred by July's heat, gridded mesh
of the screen door behind us, we remember this:

coloring books and crayons, drawing lines
to fill the space between one dot and the next,

grown-ups climbing the steps,
the pressure of air and the sound

of catching one's breath
as the door pulled itself shut.

Try to picture Grandpa in the garage,
slouched in the driver's seat,

hands spread over the wheel,
every window closed.

A few yards away, crayons gripped in our fingers,
we flattened colored wax into the paper's soft pulp,

unveiling stems and flowers line by line,
until finally, an array of petals

emerged from the white pages
and our hands stopped moving.

The Slow Passage to Anacostia

The X2 pulls to the corner, opens its tired jaw,
    then pushes ahead lurch by lurch
        into the resistance of H Street: dusk
sinking into sidewalks and take-out delis,
    hot dog vendors in empty lots,
        liquor store cashiers sealed behind glass.
Headphones spill faint rhythms
    into the bus's half-silence,
        the engine's steady hum
drones on pavement,
    and no one speaks above the clink
        of coins in the machine
until one man's voice pierces the air,
    cursing the slow passage to Anacostia,
        cursing left turns and lights fading to yellow.
No one lifts an eye except
    to gaze through scratched windows.
        Outside, the usual kids strut,
shout their own praises, stream off
    the football field or out of church.
        One car radio blares rap at a stoplight.
And here, this man's voice is a cry of longing
    to which no one listens—
        a cry of stasis, of unlit bus stops

and forsaken destinations, of the tense space
   between a man and woman
      waiting on a winter day.
Still, the X2 follows H Street all the way
   to the city's edge until something pulls
      its wheels like a magnet
back into the gridded patterns of Northeast,
   where this man's cry lingers like a vibration
      caught between the hum and the ear.

Midnight, Waiting for the Last Train

Before you can look away, he curls his lips
and locks your gaze to begin his story:

One time, I pulled out a gun
and nailed a girl on the train.

You keep your hands in your pockets,
your eyes on the black tunnel,
the escalator grumbling down step by step.

Two drunk kids descend to the platform,
shrill voices resonating on bare tracks,
filling the vast silence of the vaulted ceiling.

Have you ever been so scared
you couldn't say a word without stuttering?

A girl cartwheels along the tiled floor.
When the train's headlights flash into the station,
you thank God for the slight breeze, the ding
of doors sliding open, blinking red lights.

The man follows you into the empty car,
tells you how he slipped his fingers
under the girl's shirt, pressed the cold gun
against her thigh. He rests his palms
on the wall behind you. *I was sweating*,
he says, his breath shadowing your face,
his knees vibrating against yours.

In the next car, a girl climbs the silver bars,
swinging her legs up to the ceiling.

You grit your teeth
to brace for the long ride home.

Languages I Have Learned

1. Calligraphy
I remember each letter,
lines on paper, dip of nib in black ink,
ascending letters and descending,
the *t* stopping midway toward the height of the *h*,
the unruly *s*, the dramatic capitals
casting their weight over a whole line.

O italic, italic, I remember the seven-degree slant,
the angle of the *o* and how to make a perfect circle
with two half-ovals, I remember leaning into it,
feeling each letter in my hand,
how each word became a shape of its own.

The strained fingers, bent shoulders, hand cramps
relieved by stretching all five fingers
and clamping them again.

2. Drumming and Dance
Bare feet on the floor
answering the rhythm called out
by two hands on a drum

every muscle in my body
working at once

leaning forward to see the world
from closer to the ground

sometimes a chant would come
chanting voices blending into chanting drums

sometimes my whole body was off the ground

sometimes I pushed deeper into it
pushed my way down the floor
to kneel before the drums

the body aches
the skin opening on my feet
the sweat the make-up the head wrap
the lappa knotted at my hip
and hitched to my knees

the circle around a solo dancer
or the still breath of being that dancer
time suspended between me and the drum

Music—Unlike Poetry—

is a direct expression of the soul,
    said my father, as if this were a given fact.

Maybe he was right, after all. I know I stumble

    trying to fit the shapes inside me
        into the curves of "a," the stem of "L"—

but sometimes I feel the words well up

    in the narrow space
        between spine and ribs

and that's the deepest me, rising

    from complete chaos. You know,
        some of us live at a slant,

arms up and knees bent, waiting

    for vibration or fever,
        something to shake loose the soul,

let it spill over the edges of the page.

V

MY FATHER'S SHADOW

Walden Pond, before Dusk

I couldn't tell where water ended and sky began,
hoped if I stared hard enough,
your face would emerge
from the blurred darkness
like coming up from the basement,
wiping your sweat with a towel—

but the descending fog revealed only
a line of trees on each side of the pond,
angling toward where the horizon should be.

Did entering death resemble this?
Mist swirling so you couldn't see
where you were headed, while behind you
lay everywhere you'd ever been?

Across my field of vision
flew six black spots in a line.

I knew them as birds
only because they were in the air
before landing one by one
on what must have been water.

The Clouds Barely Make It

You come to me in the ocean,
in the fleeting manner of a fish—
a flash of life rising from the sea,
returning just as quickly,
so I might think I imagined it.

That's how it's been all these months,
looking for you everywhere. Sometimes
I almost feel the pressure
of your hand on mine.
Sometimes I can't feel you at all.

Sometimes I run into you in a dream—
I turn a corner and there you are,
on your way somewhere,
alive and intact,
warm as a father.

Just yesterday, waiting for a wave
to lift me into weightlessness,
I heard something huge
leap out of the water,
a dolphin or a great fish.

Turning, I looked hard into that planar ripple
the ocean takes on in late morning sun.
No trace. But it must have been you,
always behind me, hidden
by some trick of vision.

Maybe I believe this.
All I know is that these days
the clouds barely make it up to the sky—
they hunker down in close arcs,
encircling the hard angles of roofs.

These days, the water is so clear
coursing over my knuckles,
it seems to smooth the creases of my skin,
imprinting my five fingers on the surface
like a child's hand in paint.

And if I look down,
that dark shape on the ocean floor
is my own shadow.

These days, if I stand in a wave
as it breaks, the water clouds
and eddies about me, each swish
undoing the clarity of my shadow,
the liquid cast of my hand.

The Life Edge

for Luna, an orca that resided in Nootka Sound, British
Columbia, 2001–2006, and for the Mowachaht-Muchalaht
First Nation, which claimed him as an ancestor

Luna comes when his people chant,
beckon him away from the ocean.
He bursts out of dark water—

sleek black, sleek white,
all body and fins,
he nuzzles the edges of canoes.

Torn between the wide ocean and the finite Sound,
between his orca kin and his tribe's ancestral hum
intertwined with his own wave-cutting rhythm,

he is like my father, in death—

sometimes stays close to the life edge
as if to come back to our constant clamor,
and sometimes disappears into the depths.

Does Luna crave those moments of solitude,
night-swimming, fins sliding through waves,
breaking through the surface?

He goes all the way to the mouth
of the ocean, pauses, then turns back
into the embrace of familiar waters.

Nocturnal Life

Lately, my grief has turned
to an obsession with your nocturnal life—
all the nights you slept,
all the mornings you awoke—
a life's worth of dreams.

Remember, you were always speaking
or on the cusp of another word.
I'd begin an utterance
and your voice would break in.

Evenings, the piano resounded
with your renderings
of Nachtmusik or Chopin—
your lips set, torso lifting and lowering,
foot on the pedal.

If I could envision
your soundless inner life—
if I could splice your dreams together
into one seamless reel
tracing the course of your subconscious
from childhood's gilded chords
to your last open-hearted day,

would I understand the silence
I hear from you now?

Grief

When the grief began to lift,
I didn't want it to go,

didn't want to separate *mother*
into present tense and *father* into past.

I wanted your death to remain shocking,
your blood always on the t-shirt,

your voice on the machine
reaching out to us from the other side.

I wanted to hold on to our last conversation—
how I carried the phone through each doorway,

describing the polished corners of my new home,
how each room hinged to another,

how sun poured through the glass,
casting angles of light on wooden floors,

and beyond my window, the graceful twist
of a live oak in the yard.

I never wanted to lose your intonation.
The rise and fall of your questions.

Every Gnarled Inch

for a live oak

Something about the way the trunk splits,
carving its shape in two directions
as if upward were not enough,

the way it juts out from the sidewalk,
leaning over the street
like the slant of an A,
parallel to nothing.

Something about the crook of the branches,
trunk-thick and nearly horizontal,
each with a slight dip, a shallow
to hold water from a day's rain,

how it grounds itself, how the base broadens
and flares into a pleated skirt of roots
creeping farther and farther out,
molding to the slope of earth.

Something about the curve
of the trunk, twisting and inclining,
maintaining its gesture
in spite of time, in spite of us,

as if it had struggled to grow
every gnarled inch,
now etched solid against air.

The Armoire

What did I know of wood then?
Maple or pine—I noticed only the varnish,
the color of honey with a core of yellow
somewhere deep within. And the key
that stayed always in the keyhole,
the kind I could hook my finger into,
notched grooves that would turn and open
the great doors to our family's history
embedded in the shelves of old books.

There in five gold-trimmed volumes was Shakespeare
and a midnight-blue edition of *Arabian Nights,*
cloaked in moonlit orange skies.
Mark Twain, Tolstoy, *The Sun Also Rises*—

I didn't read them. Just touched the bindings,
noted the slant of type or the paper's fiber,
maybe opened a cover to find an inscription,
an ex libris pasted inside, inked with your signature.

So many things have become important
and meaningless at the same time: the shape
of an apostrophe and its proper location,
the space between words on a page,
the slight cross or dot to mark
a particular letter, the clarity of vowel sounds.

Now that the maple leaves have reddened
and fallen into the coming winter,
pine needles stiffened on their branches,
now that the winters stretch endlessly before us,
what good is it to distinguish
one brittle leaf from another?

If I could go there,
if I could tilt the books back one at a time
and read the words imprinted on each spine,
somewhere in the slight indentation
of each letter, I might find
a resting place. With my thumb,
I might feel the smooth lines of death
in the thickness of the wood,
some assurance that where you are now
reflects the fluidity of that grain,
forever rearranging its swirls of gold.

Notes

"Juliek's Violin" — The italicized phrase is from *Night*, a Holocaust memoir by Nobel Peace Laureate Elie Wiesel (*The Night Trilogy*, Hill and Wang, 1987, p. 99). This poem describes the "death march" that Wiesel and his fellow concentration camp inmates, including his friend Juliek, were forced to take at the end of World War II. As Allied Forces began to close in, Nazi authorities began moving prisoners en masse toward Germany's interior, in a desperate attempt to prevent the Allies from discovering the concentration camps and liberating the prisoners.

"The Words of the Script" — The italicized lines are from Shakespeare's *King Lear*.

"The Line between River and Ocean" — Cape Fear, North Carolina, is where the Cape Fear River meets the Atlantic Ocean.

"Gliding Through This Place" — Sadako Sasaki was a Japanese girl who contracted leukemia as a result of exposure to the atomic bomb that was dropped on Hiroshima by the United States at the end of World War II. She died at the age of 12 from the disease. Her courage inspired her friends to start a peace movement, and she became a symbol of the importance of a nuclear-free world. A statue of her stands in Hiroshima as well as in Seattle. Her story was memorialized for the English-speaking audience in Eleanor Coerr's 1977 children's book *Sadako and the Thousand Paper Cranes*. For details about Sadako's life and the horrific effects of the bombing, I relied on Masamoto Nasu's *Children of the Paper Crane: The Story of Sadako Sasaki and Her Struggle with the A-Bomb Disease* (M. E. Sharpe, 1991).

"Radiance" – In Ray Bradbury's science fiction story "All Summer in a Day," Margot lives on the planet Venus, where the sun comes out only once every seven years.

"In the Wadi" – This poem was inspired by Wadi Rum, in southern Jordan.

"Smoke" – This poem describes the smoking of a *sheesha*, or water pipe.

"The Slow Ferry" – When I traveled between Jordan and Egypt, there were two options: "the fast ferry" or "the slow ferry."

"Moulid: Night of the Prophet" – A *moulid* is a celebration of a prophet that involves a multi-day grand street festival. The "big night" (described in this poem) is a culmination of the festival with religious music and chants lasting through the night. There are *moulids* for different prophets that occur throughout the year in various parts of Egypt.

"The Unfinished Obelisk" – A famous site in Upper Egypt.

"In the Valley of the Kings" – The Valley of the Kings is also a famous site in Upper Egypt, where many prominent kings and pharaohs were buried, possibly including Ramses I and II.

"Finding the Way" – "This hidden town" refers to Wilmington, North Carolina.

"In Plié" – For Melvin Deal, director of African Heritage Dancers and Drummers, in Washington, D.C.

"The Slow Passage to Anacostia" – Anacostia is a neighborhood in Washington, D.C., separated from the rest of the city by the Anacostia River.

"The Life Edge" – Luna was an orca that became separated from its family at a young age and lived alone for several years in Nootka Sound, near Vancouver Island, which is highly unusual for this social animal. When Luna was discovered in the sound in 2001, the local Inuit tribe, the Mowachaht/ Muchalaht First Nation, claimed him as their former chief, who had recently died and promised to come back as an orca. In 2004, a confrontation ensued between the tribespeople—

who wanted Luna to remain free and undisturbed—and Canadian fishery authorities, who wanted to trap him and return him to his family. To lure Luna away from the trap, the tribespeople went out in canoes chanting day after day, and Luna followed them. Eventually, the authorities gave up their efforts. Luna remained in Nootka Sound until 2006, when he was accidentally struck and killed by a boat propeller. Michael Parfit's article "Whale of a Tale" (*Smithsonian* magazine, November 2004), was very useful in writing this poem. In 2011, a documentary film about the story, called *The Whale,* was released in the United States.

More Poetry from Gival Press

12: Sonnets for the Zodiac

by John Gosslee; French translation by Elizabeth D. Watson, Spanish translation by Jose M. Guerrero

ISBN 13: 978-1-928589-58-7, $15

"In John Gosslee's debut collection, *12*, he chisels to perfection sonnets that masterfully treat the characters of the western zodiac...."
— Carolyn Kreiter-Foronda, Poet Laureate of Virginia, 2006-2008

Adamah: Poème

by Céline Zins; translation by Peter Schulman

ISBN 13: 978-1-928589-46-4, $15

2010 Honorable Mention — Paris Book Festival for Poetry
This bilingual (French/English) collection by an eminent French poet/writer is adeptly translated in this premiere edition.

Bones Washed With Wine: Flint Shards from Sussex and Bliss

by Jeff Mann

ISBN 13: 978-1-928589-14-3, $15

Includes the 1999 Gival Press Poetry Award winning collection. Jeff Mann is "a poet to treasure both for the wealth of his language and the generosity of his spirit." — Edward Falco, author of *Acid*

Canciones para sola cuerda / Songs for a Single String

by Jesús Gardea; English translation by Robert L. Giron

ISBN 13: 978-1-928589-09-9, $15

Finalist for the 2003 Violet Crown Book Award — Literary Prose & Poetry.

Love poems, with echoes of Neruda à la Mexicana, Gardea writes about the primeval quest for the perfect woman.

Dervish

by Gerard Wozek

ISBN 13: 978-1-928589-11-2, $15

Winner of the 2000 Gival Press Poetry Award / Finalist for the 2002 Violet Crown Book Award — Literary Prose & Poetry. "By jove, these poems shimmer." — Gerry Gomez Pearlberg, author of *Mr. Bluebird*

The Great Canopy

by Paula Goldman

ISBN 13: 978-1-928589-31-0, $15

Winner of the 2004 Gival Press Poetry Award / 2006 Independent Publisher Book Award — Honorable Mention for Poetry
"Under this canopy we experience the physicality of the body through Goldman's wonderfully muscular verse as well the analytics of a mind that tackles the meaning of Orpheus or the notion of desire." — Richard Jackson, author of *Half Lives*

Grip

by Yvette Neisser Moreno

ISBN 13: 978-1-928589 -76-1, $15

Winner of the 2011 Gival Press Poetry Award
"Yvette Neisser Moreno's poems shimmer in that mysterious space between rib and spine, body and sky, farewell and departure." — Barbara Goldberg

Honey
by Richard Carr
ISBN 13: 978-1-928589-45-7, $15

Winner of the 2007 Gival Press Poetry Award / 2008 Finalist — ForeWord Magazine Book Award for Poetry

"*Honey* is a tour de force. Comprised of 100 electrifying microsonnets . . . The whole sequence creates a narrative that becomes, like the Hapax Legomenon, a form that occurs only once in a literature." — Barbara Louise Ungar, author of *The Origin of the Milky Way*

Let Orpheus Take Your Hand
by George Klawitter
ISBN 13: 978-1-928589-16-7, $15

Winner of the 2001 Gival Press Poetry Award

A thought provoking work that mixes the spiritual with stealthy desire, with Orpheus leading us out of the pit.

Metamorphosis of the Serpent God
by Robert L. Giron
ISBN 13: 978-1-928589-07-5, $12

This collection "...embraces the past and the present, ethnic and sexual identity, themes both mythical and personal." — *The Midwest Book Review*

Museum of False Starts
by Chip Livingston
ISBN 13: 978-1-928589-49-5, $15

Livingston - a "mixed blood" poet - presents a new approach to poetry through his experience.

"...Chip Livingston makes the ordinary exotic, erotic and extraordinary." — Ai

On the Altar of Greece

by Donna J. Gelagotis Lee

ISBN 13: 978-1-92-8589-36-5, $15

Winner of the 2005 Gival Press Poetry Award / 2007 Eric Hoffer Book Award: Notable for Art Category

"…*On the Altar of Greece* is like a good travel guide: it transforms reader into visitor and nearly into resident. It takes the visitor to the authentic places that few tourists find, places delightful yet still surprising, safe yet unexpected…" — Simmons B. Buntin, editor of *Terrain.org Blog*

On the Tongue

by Jeff Mann

ISBN 13: 978-1-928589-35-8, $15

"…These poems are …nothing short of extraordinary." — Trebor Healey, author of *Sweet Son of Pan*

The Nature Sonnets

by Jill Williams

ISBN 13: 978-1-928589-10-5, $8^{95}

An innovative collection of sonnets that speaks to the cycle of nature and life, crafted with wit and clarity. "Refreshing and pleasing." — Miles David Moore, author of *The Bears of Paris*

The Origin of the Milky Way

by Barbara Louise Ungar

ISBN 13: 978-1-928589-39-6, $15

Winner of the 2006 Gival Press Poetry Award / 2007 Adirondack Literary Award for the Best Book of Poetry / 2008 Eric Hoffer Award — Notable for Poetry / Silver 2008 Independent Publisher Book Award for Poetry

"...a fearless, unflinching collection about birth and motherhood, the transformation of bodies. Ungar's poems are honestly brutal, candidly tender. Their primal immediacy and intense intimacy are realized through her dazzling sense of craft. Ungar delivers a wonderful, sensuous, visceral poetry." — Denise Duhamel

Poetic Voices Without Borders

edited by Robert L. Giron

ISBN 13: 978-1-928589-30-3, $20

2006 Writer's Notes Magazine Book Award — Notable for Art / 2006 Independent Publisher Book Award — Honorable Mention for Anthology

An international anthology of poetry in English, French, and Spanish, including work by Grace Cavalieri, Jewell Gomez, Joy Harjo, Peter Klappert, Jaime Manrique, C.M. Mayo, E. Ethelbert Miller, Richard Peabody, Myra Sklarew and many others.

Poetic Voices Without Borders 2

edited by Robert L. Giron

ISBN 13: 978-1-928589-43-3, $20

Winner 2009 National Best Book Award for Anthologies / Runner-Up 2009 London Book Festival Award for Poetry / 2009 San Francisco Book Festival — Honorable Mention for Poetry.

Featuring poets Grace Cavalieri, Rita Dove, Dana Gioia, Joy Harjo, Peter Klappert, Philip Levine, Gloria Vando, and many other fine poets in English, French, and Spanish.

Prosody in England and Elsewhere: A Comparative Approach

by Leonardo Malcovati

ISBN 13: 978-1-928589-26-6, $20

The perfect tool for the poet but written for a non-specialist audience.

Protection
by Gregg Shapiro
ISBN 13: 978-1-928589-41-9, $15

"Gregg Shapiro's stunning debut marks the arrival of a new master poet on the scene. His work blows me away." — Greg Herren, author of *Mardi Gras Mambo*

Psaltery and Serpentines
by Cecilia Martínez-Gil
ISBN 13: 978-1-928589-52-5, $15

Winner of the 2009 Gival Press Poetry Award / Runner-Up 2010 Los Angeles Book Festival Award for Poetry / Finalist 2010 National Best Book Award for Poetry / Finalist 2010 ForeWord Reviews Book of the Year Award for Poetry
"This is a luscious and lustrous collection of poems..." — Gail Wronsky

The Refugee
by Vladimir Levchev
ISBN 13: 978-1-928589-57-0, $15

Translated from Bulgarian with Alicia Suskin and Henry Taylor.
"We are in the presence of a large spirit who writes in the greatest tradition of European masters." — Grace Cavalieri

The Silent Art
by Clifford Bernier
ISBN 13: 978-1-928589-62-4, $15

Winner of the 2010 Gival Press Poetry Award
"*The Silent Art* takes us on a journey through countries, landscapes, musical forms and states of mind. Rivers flow through these places to the beat of conga drums, the wail of an alto sax." — Judith Valente

Songs for the Spirit

by Robert L. Giron

ISBN 13: 978-1-928589-08-2, $16^{95}

A psalter for the reader who is not religious but who is spiritually inclined. "This is an extraordinary book." — John Shelby Spong

Sweet to Burn

by Beverly Burch

ISBN 13: 978-1-928589-23-5, $15

Winner of the 2004 Lambda Literary Award for Lesbian Poetry / Winner of the 2003 Gival Press Poetry Award
"Novelistic in scope, but packing the emotional intensity of lyric poetry..." — Eloise Klein Healy, author of *Passing*

Tickets to a Closing Play

by Janet I. Buck

ISBN 13: 978-1-928589-25-9, $15

Winner of the 2002 Gival Press Poetry Award
"...this rich and vibrant collection of poetry [is] not only serious and insightful, but a sheer delight to read." — Jane Butkin Roth, editor of *We Used to Be Wives: Divorce Unveiled Through Poetry*

Voyeur

by Rich Murphy

ISBN 13: 978-1-928589-48-8, $15

Winner of the 2008 Gival Press Poetry Award / Winner of the 2009 Los Angeles Book Festival Award for Poetry / Honorable Mention: 2009 London Book Festival for Poetry & 2009 New England Book Festival for Poetry

"*Voyeur* is a work of vision and virtuosity. Concerned with relationships, marriage, sex and power, the poetry is dense, rapid, dazzling, the voice commanding, the speaker charismatic…spectacular." — Richard Carr

Where a Poet Ought Not / Où c'qui faut pas
by G. Tod Slone
(in English and French)
ISBN 13: 978-1-928589-42-6, $15

Poems inspired by French poets Léo Ferré and François Villon and the Québec poet Raymond Lévesque in what Slone characterizes as a need to speak up. "In other words, a poet should speak the truth as he sees it and fight his damnedest to overcome all the forces encouraging not to."

For a list of poetry published by Gival Press, please visit: *www.givalpress.com*

Books are available from BookMasters, Ingram, the Internet, and other outlets.
or write

Gival Press, LLC
PO Box 3812
Arlington, VA 22203
703.351.0079